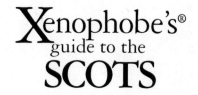

Xenophobe's®
guide to the
SCOTS

David Ross

D0715321

Oval Books

Xenophobe's Guides
5 St. John's Buildings
Canterbury Crescent
London SW9 7QH
United Kingdom

Telephone: +44 (0)20 7733 8585
E-mail: info@ovalbooks.com
Web site: www.xenophobes.com

First printed 1999
New edition 2009
Reprinted/updated 2000, 2001, 2002, 2004,
2006, 2009, 2011

Editor – Catriona Tulloch Scott
Series Editor – Anne Tauté

Cover designer – Jim Wire & Vicki Towers
Printer – CPI Antony Rowe, Wiltshire

Acknowledgement and thanks are
given to Alexander Rae for his
witty contributions.

ePub ISBN: 9781908120816
Mobi ISBN: 9781908120823
Print ISBN: 9781906042479

Contents

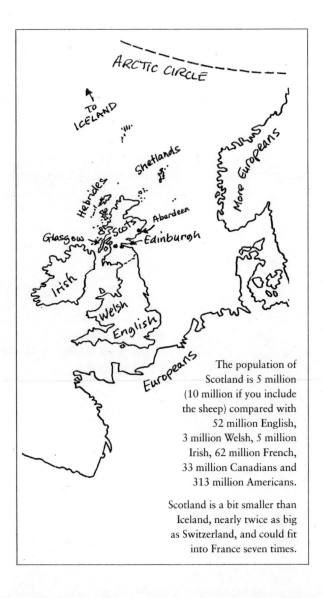

ARCTIC CIRCLE

TO ICELAND

Shetlands

Hebrides

More Europeans

Scots

Aberdeen

Glasgow

Edinburgh

Irish

Welsh

English

Europeans

The population of Scotland is 5 million (10 million if you include the sheep) compared with 52 million English, 3 million Welsh, 5 million Irish, 62 million French, 33 million Canadians and 313 million Americans.

Scotland is a bit smaller than Iceland, nearly twice as big as Switzerland, and could fit into France seven times.

Nationalism & Identity

Forewarned

If there is one characteristic that defines the Scots it is that they are different. Not better or worse than anyone else, but definitely not to be confused with any other nation. A great deal of effort is put into being distinctive. Some people think this is all to do with the tourism industry, but they are quite wrong. The Scots do it entirely for their own satisfaction.

Living as they do on the north-western edge of Europe, the Scots have evolved their own way of doing things, and take great pride in it. Being Scottish is not simple and straightforward, and for many Scots perfecting their Scottishness is a lifetime's activity.

> **Being Scottish is not simple and straightforward. For many Scots perfecting their Scottishness is a lifetime's activity.**

This may lead you to think that the Scots are a nation addicted to showing off and boasting. Nothing could be further from the truth – they just want you to appreciate the fact that they are people who dance to their own particular tune. Knowing this enables you to appreciate their finer points: this is the essence of judgement, and all Scots are judges at heart.

The Scots have a very sustained and steady sense of their own worth, and they don't mind who knows it. Apart from such things as whisky, tartan, bagpipe music and Dundee cake, they have given the world the bicycle, gas for lighting, the first effective steam engine, the pneumatic tyre, chloroform, the telephone, television, penicillin, the ultra-sound scanner, paraffin, the mackintosh, the milking machine, the water softener, Dolly the cloned sheep... and if you didn't know this, they'll be glad to enlighten you. This is not a reticent, withdrawn, sorry-we've-bothered-you set of people.

Exported Scots

About 5 million Scots live in Scotland but over the past few centuries 30 million Scots have been scattered to the four corners of the earth. There are special nuclei, 'little Scotlands', in South Carolina, Eastern Canada, the South Island of New Zealand – and in the BBC. Yet though they have been Americans, Canadians or New Zealanders for ten generations, they know deep down in their hearts that they are really Scots.

> **Even if they have been Americans, Canadians or New Zealanders for ten generations they know deep down in their hearts that they are really Scots.**

Many with only tenuous reasons for attachment are drawn by sentiment. Forebears of the artist Whistler, whose middle name was McNeill, hailed from a small island on the west coast of Scotland and his American descendants make regular visits 'home'.

Scots, it seems, are often keen to leave their country, then spend the rest of their lives attending Caledonian Society Meetings, celebrating with haggis and singing mawkishly sentimental songs, with tears in their eyes, about their 'Highland home far across the sea'. They always have a 'Highland home far across the sea', even if they came from Glasgow.

How they see others

Non-Scots are divided into two main groups:

    1. The English
    2. The Rest

If you belong among The Rest, you have a head start.

The Scots generally find strangers fascinating, and many are the tales recounted by the lonely traveller of how he was welcomed with open arms in some remote Scottish glen. As long as he wasn't English of course.

Americans are liked partly because many of the Americans who come to Scotland are of Scots ancestry, but more because of their perceived uncomplicated open-ness and generosity. Canadians are equally popular, if not more so, because they are even more likely to be just a few generations away from being Scottish themselves.

> **Scots are often keen to leave their country, then sing sentimental songs about their 'Highland home across the sea'.**

The Scots also like Europeans, especially those from Scandinavia, who they see as fellow-Northerners, sharing virtues that combine individualism and community spirit, and enduring the same testing weather conditions. They particularly admire vibrant and fully independent countries whose populations are not much bigger, or perhaps even smaller, than their own – like Denmark, Switzerland and, of course, Ireland, that other Celtic nation, so similar in many ways yet so different in certain fundamentals. From the great mixer-blender of history, the Irish have emerged with fire on the outside and steel inside. The Scots are the exact opposite.

The 'Auld Alliance'

The ability of the Scots to get on with anyone is amply proven by the fact that throughout history they have always managed to maintain an alliance with the French – the Auld Alliance – a feat not even attempted by any other European culture. The unkind might suggest that the only thing the Scots and the French have in common is that both believe that any race that dislikes the English couldn't be all bad, but this is a vile rumour.

> 66 They have always managed to maintain an alliance with the French – a feat not even attempted by any other European culture. 99

The 'Auld Enemy'

The Scots have given the world so much, usually without asking whether it wanted it, but they are obliged to accept that the main conduit of innovation from outside – political, social, cultural, industrial – has always been that large country to the South, the 'Auld Enemy', England. Always more numerous, always richer, always ready to assert their superiority, the English have been thorns in the Scottish flesh for a thousand years. The Scots have learned their pride, their nationality, their characteristics good and bad, chiefly at the hands of the English, often violently. They are not about to forgive them for it.

> **The Scots have learned their pride, their nationality their characteristics good and bad chiefly at the hands of the English. They are not about to forgive them for it.**

When God created Scotland, says a favourite Scottish story, he looked down on it with great satisfaction. Finally he called the archangel Gabriel to have a look. "Just see," He said. "This is the best yet. Fine mountains, brave men, lovely women, nice cool weather. And I've given them beautiful music and a special drink, called whisky. Try some." Gabriel took an appreciative sip. "Excellent," he said. "But haven't you perhaps been too generous? Won't they be spoiled? Should there not be some drawback?" And God said: "Just wait till you see the neighbours I'm giving them."

A concern shared by the Scots is that, as a nation, their behaviour is the product of a deep sense of being a lesser nation. A country cannot give up its independent nationhood, as the Scots did in 1707, without a few qualms and a sharp sense of what was being lost. Even before that, Scotland was twice turned into a province of England (under Edward I, the 'Hammer of the Scots', and under Oliver Cromwell). Both times, independence was reclaimed. The Scots are used to picking themselves up and starting again – you can see this process at work in the country's regular ability to reach the World Cup Finals in soccer, only to be knocked out in the first round.

> **66 The Scots have always had to shout to make their voices heard and their presence known. 99**

However, any fear of inferiority is misplaced. Like a small broadcasting station whose wavebands are jammed by another, the Scots have always had to shout to make their voices heard and their presence known. Otherwise the stifling proximity of England would have silenced them long ago and Scotland would be a sort of northern extension of Northumberland.

Scots are quick to sense patronage and arrogance in an English accent, especially a 'posh' one. It brings out the latent prickliness in the Scottish character. (It's not for nothing that the national emblem is the thistle.) They label the English as snobbish, class-ridden and self-satisfied. The two nations have been eyeball to

6

eyeball for so long that what each sees of the other is more caricature than reality. The reality is that for 250 years the Scots and the English have not fought each other on any field more bloody than a sports ground.

Most English people are blithely unaware of how much the Scots resent the English habit of using the terms 'England' and 'Britain' as if they were one and the same. And what annoys the Scots even more is when it's a Scottish success that is being celebrated at, say, an international sporting event, and the English claim it as British.

> 66 English people are blithely unaware of how much the Scots resent the use of 'England and Britain as if they were one and the same. 99

This goes some way to explain why thousands of Scots will be turning cartwheels if Iraq has beaten England at lacrosse or real tennis. Scots who have never seen a game of cricket have been known to go on week-long binges to celebrate the fact that some minuscule third-world country has managed to beat England at its national sport.

How they see themselves

The Scots like to feel that they are a rather flamboyant and colourful people – tartan inside as well as out.

They see themselves as clever and well-educated. They respect knowledge and like to think that they possess plenty of it. In Scotland there is nothing wrong with being clever, so long as you show it by words or actions rather than brag about it. To say of someone that "he has a good conceit of himself" is neither praise nor blame, just a statement of fact.

Scottish cleverness is not entirely mythical. A civil servant from Edinburgh made his first visit to see his superiors in London. When he came back, he was asked, "How did you like the English?" "I don't know," he replied. "I only met heads of departments."

> **A Scotsman likes to feel that, almost by instinct, he could guddle a trout or gralloch a deer.**

They also cherish their pragmatic, practical streak. A Scots housewife is, virtually by definition, tidy, able to sew cushions or bake a cake, and make her own breakfast marmalade. She may still darn her children's socks and she's sure to know six different ways of using up yesterday's cold potatoes. A Scotsman likes to feel that, almost by instinct, he could guddle a trout (palm it out of the water) or gralloch a deer (disembowel it with his knife), even if he spends his day designing software or driving a bus.

The Scots view themselves as independent-minded yet communally spirited, humorous and warm-hearted. A favourite word for themselves is 'kindly' which means friendly, good-humoured, easy-going, willing to share what little one has, thinking well of others, being part of the community. Well, every nation has an ideal to aspire to, and the Scots are no exception.

How they see each other

Scots identify one another by geography. When Scot meets Scot outside Scotland, only their shared Scottishness matters: they are fellow-countryfolk, though the cordiality will be all the greater if both are from Ayrshire, or Auchtermuchty.

At home they are rivals. A whole mental catalogue of social reference points is held in readiness. The Scots are an analytical people and never take anything at face value. Their most severe criticisms are reserved for one another. This is not a matter of high standards, but of sheer competitiveness, and even jealousy. Nothing can beat the vituperative energy with which small, schismatic Presbyterian sects excommunicate those who defy their narrow code. This happened to a one-time Lord Chancellor, who was expelled from membership of the Free Presbyterian Church because he ventured to attend the funeral of a friend who was Roman Catholic.

> **❝ When Scot meets Scot outside Scotland, only their shared Scottishness matters. At home they are rivals. ❞**

The rivalry between Edinburgh and Glasgow is famous. After their side won the European Cup in Lisbon, two Glasgow Celtic fans were setting off to hitch-hike home to Scotland when a car drew up. "Like a lift? We're going to Edinburgh," said the driver. "That's no good," they said, "We're going to Glasgow."

Edinburgh folk regard Glasgow as a trollop of a town, brash, noisy and vulgar. The Glaswegians retaliate with their view of the typical Edinburgher, "all fur coat and no knickers". A character in a story by Neil Munro (1863–1930) says: "All the wise men in Glasgow come from the East – that's to say they come from Edinburgh." "Yes," replies a Glaswegian, "and the wiser they are, the quicker they come."

There are other rivalries, including that between the Highlanders and the Lowlanders. Contrary to what many suppose, the mix of Celtic and pre-Celtic peoples, Nordic settlers, Anglo-Saxons, and Flemings is shared by them both. Thus the differences are cultural rather than ethnic, and used to be underlined by the fact that Gaelic, once the language of the whole country, continued for centuries to be spoken in the Highlands. This does not prevent the Highlanders from regarding the Lowlanders as being regimented urbanites little more civilised than the English. Not to be outdone, the Lowlanders consider the Highlanders to be a crowd of lazy, dreamy, feckless subsidy-junkies. It was obviously not a Highlander who composed 'The Crofter's Prayer':

> Oh, that the peats would cut themselves,
> The fish jump on the shore;

> **The Highlanders regard the Lowlanders as being regimented urbanites little more civilised than the English.**

And that I in my bed could always lie
And sleep for evermore.

Competition and rivalry come right down to local level, and neighbouring towns often have highly un-neighbourly things to say about each other. Even within a town, people form tribal divisions. In the Orkney capital of Kirkwall, the annual 'Ba' (ball) game' is fought out on New Year's Day between two sections of the town, the 'Uppies' and the 'Doonies', and no Uppie would ever dream of siding with the opposition, any more than would a Doonie.

The harshest judgements, however, fall on football referees who are invariably assumed by supporters of the losing team to be in diabolic conspiracy with the other side. They frequently have to sneak from the ground with their coat over their heads.

How others see them

Foreigners believe that the average Scotsman is tall, with legs like tree-trunks and arms like Popeye's just after a can of spinach. He is supposedly prodigiously strong from caber tossing, has a red beard, a red nose and wears a bright red tartan kilt and a tweed jacket that would tear the skin off a lesser mortal in seconds. He drinks whisky for breakfast and eats nothing but porridge, haggis and salmon. He also likes to shout and fight a lot.

As everyone knows, racial stereotypes are notoriously inaccurate. In this case, however, the stereotype is an uncannily true thumbnail sketch of every second person you meet walking down Glasgow's Sauchiehall Street on a Saturday night. The bit about the shouting and fighting is, anyway.

> **To the English the average Scotsman is a short, unshaven football supporter wearing a Scotland scarf which he holds out at arms' length as if waiting for it to dry.**

To the English (who, however else they are viewed by the Scots, are not considered foreigners) the average Scotsman is a short, unshaven football supporter wearing a Scotland scarf which he holds out at arms' length as if waiting for it to dry. By profession he is either a trades union negotiator or a comedian. He eats nothing but fish and chips, drinks whisky and likes to shout and fight a lot.

To many other peoples (except the French), the Scots are English. They can't understand what all the fuss is about when they say something friendly like: "I would like to say how much I admire you English and your excellent football teams." After this they think that the average Scotsman likes to shout and fight a lot.

The French who have been intimately connected with the Scots for centuries have a saying '*fier comme un Ecossais*' – as proud as a Scot. The Germans in the First World War called the kilted Scottish regiments 'the ladies from Hell'.

How they would like to be seen

The Scots would like to be seen by others as they see themselves. Failing that, the Scotsman of popular imagination – a tartan-swathed figure of heroic strength, red-haired, red-bearded and spoiling for a fight – is an image that Scots are quite happy to accept, particularly the stocky, unfit, balding ones.

Character

The Scots are a nation of polarities: sober and wild, traditional and innovative, inhibited and emotional. It is these contradictions in the Scottish character that are exploited by Robert Louis Stevenson's Dr. Jekyll and Mr. Hyde, in which the same individual is both the kindly doctor and his fiendish alter ego.

Few people can show greater kindness and concern for misfortune than the Scots. But they can also exhibit a brusqueness, a touch of aggressiveness, as if they feel that the world is a hostile place and they must square up to it.

Being canny

The Scottish characteristic of being canny, or being called canny, comes in various forms.

First there is the 'canny Scot' who thinks before he

speaks. Some Scottish silences are merely the pause before the plunge. Deep and different things lie behind this – the wish not to offend being one. Another is the desire to avoid being caught making some foolish remark. The Scots are not just sharp judges; they have long memories. One feeble utterance can mark a person down as a brainless 'numpty' for life. It's an environment in which you have to be canny yourself to survive unscathed.

> **66 The Scots are not just sharp judges; they have long memories. One feeble utterance can mark a person down as a brainless 'numpty' for life. 99**

Secondly, there is the 'too-canny Scot' who has developed an exaggerated concern not to commit himself. For him it is best not to stick out in the crowd, never to be in any way 'kenspeckle' (noticeable). 'Always be cautious before folk' is the maxim of this individual, and nothing alarms him so much as being faced with the kind of direct question that probes into what he really thinks about some issue. A look of desperation will appear, he will glance this way and that, and finally mutter "Maybe aye, maybe no". He may harbour opinions of the most extreme kind, but he would only utter them among those he knows share them.

Thirdly, and perhaps the most common perception of the canny Scot, is the prudent, careful person, and its roots lie a long way back. Before the Industrial Revolution Scotland was not a rich country. People were accustomed to making do. Nothing was wasted. Centuries of deprivation have had an influence on the national character. The Scots learned long ago to husband their resources, financial or otherwise, in order to survive bad times, worse times, and times of real trouble, as when the English invaded. Bad times were normal and easier to cope with. Good times made them nervous – sooner or later would come a day of reckoning, so they saved whatever came their way, and stowed away their bawbees in dark corners.

> **There is a national impulse, lurking just beneath the surface, to be contradictory.**

Even the Scots concede that this prudent kind of 'canny' can be taken too far, as in the apocryphal story of a host greeting an unexpected guest with, "Come in, come in. You'll have had your tea?"

Being thrawn

There is a national impulse, lurking just beneath the surface, to be contradictory. It is a form of bloody-mindedness for which the Scots have their own term – 'thrawn'. This virtually untranslatable word combines obstinacy, assertiveness, and more than a hint of wil-ful perversity. It is one of the steely elements in the Scottish character.

What it means in practice is that a Scot will take

pleasure in deliberately uttering the opposite of what has just been said, or doing something quite unexpected, just for the sake of it. And once the Scots get an idea into their heads, even if subsequently proved false, it can be very difficult to remove it.

Being pawky and being dour

Two words characterise the Scots. One is 'pawky', the other is 'dour'. They mean opposite things. Pawky is defined as 'tricky, artful; dryly humorous'. The pawky Scot is a person with a droll grin and a wisecrack to accompany it. 'Dour', on the other hand, means 'obstinate; austere; humourless'. The dour Scot has a grim expression, a grim mind, and a grim turn of phrase to go with it. It is a special Scottish talent to combine both characteristics within the same person.

In a display of his dour aspect a husband told his dying wife that, all right, he would allow her sister to ride beside him in the carriage to attend her funeral. "But," he added, "it'll fair spoil the day for me." The anecdote itself is a pawky one.

Hiding emotions

The Scots are not a frivolous people. Seriousness is a natural companion of the grey skies, the craggy architecture and all that porridge.

They keep their innermost feelings to themselves. They will communicate love with a pat on the shoulder or a peck on the cheek; they will tell you a joke without smiling; they will stand silent and apparently unmoved at funerals; they will say goodbye to their dearest friends without a hint of emotion. The highest form of praise ever uttered by many of them is "Not bad". Being Scottish would appear to be a heavy responsibility.

The Scottish writer John Buchan once solemnly proclaimed: "We are the most emotional nation on earth." He clearly had in mind that dangerously tempestuous surges must lie deep beneath stern Scottish countenances if they are so reluctant to let them loose.

> **66 Dangerously tempestuous surges must lie deep beneath stern Scottish countenances if they are so reluctant to let them loose. 99**

This reticence to display ordinary human vulnerability can sometimes lead to an unattractive gruffness. Some Scots can seem surly and unfriendly without meaning to, or at least without being able to help it. They have developed a challenging, brusque manner to protect the fragile, sensitive spirit within, and done it so successfully that it is never detected by others. Often such people are very surprised at this failure to perceive their marshmallow centre, and go through life feeling misunderstood and under-appreciated, becoming even more gruff as a result.

Two things can be relied upon to release Scottish inhibitions. One is being abroad. The Scot abroad is infinitely more human than at home. Surrounded by people who don't mind showing their feelings, and warmed by an unfamiliar sun, the protective shell drops off. Taciturnity is replaced by garrulity, diffidence by confidence, shyness by expansive gestures, and the picture of the flamboyant Scot gains a little more colour.

> **66 If the Scots were to shed their seriousness, they would be noisier than the Neapolitans, more dramatic than the Spaniards and wilder than the Dervishes. 99**

The other is drinking. It may take a little more alcohol to release Scottish inhibitions than it does with other people, but it works in the end.

Few Scots avoid being imbued with the national qualities of reserve and seriousness, unless they happen to be a 'character' – those who somehow escape such constraints, often saying exactly what they think in forcible terms, or even embracing people in public.

There are more characters around, in all walks of life, than you would suppose. In fact, you will come to realise that if the Scots were to shed their seriousness, they would be noisier than the Neapolitans, more dramatic than the Spaniards and wilder than the Dervishes. Their reserve is not a defence against the rest of the world: it is a necessary protective cover, rather like the lid of a nuclear reactor.

Attitudes & Values

The Calvinist legacy

For a few decades in the 17th century the Scots were possibly the most religious race on earth – fanatically so, ready to kill anyone who opposed their extreme Protestant, or Calvinist, views. Ever since, they have been winding down towards a more easy-going approach. It has taken a long time: far into the 20th century the Scottish Sunday, or Sabbath, was notorious for its extreme quiet – or dullness. A humorous versifier summed it up: '... at least, to begin the week well, let us all be unhappy on Sunday.'

It was only after the arrival of television that the Scottish Sunday cracked. Nowadays,

> **❝ You can encounter extremes of austere piety and wild behaviour, sometimes in the same individual. ❞**

anything goes, including football matches. Even, on the Isle of Lewis, last stronghold of the old Sabbatarianism, where the ferry service until recently was strictly Monday to Saturday and the only Sunday service was in church.

The Scots are still learning how to wear, more lightly than they have in the past, the formidable cloak of Calvinism, with its terrifying – or inspiring – insistence on the individual's direct responsibility to God. You can encounter extremes of austere piety and wild behaviour, sometimes in the same individual.

Where God seems very close, the Devil is never far away, and the Scots often appear to have a close relationship with both. They tell a story about the Day of Judgement, with the damned all gathered in Hell, while God looks down on them. "Lord, Lord, we didna ken (know)," they cry beseechingly. "Weel," says God, "Ye ken noo."

Today the majority of churchgoers attend the established Church of Scotland – known as the Kirk. Although Calvinist in creed, many of the modern Kirk's ideas, including the acceptance of women ministers and a relaxed view of 'gay' lifestyles, would make any old-style Presbyterian reach for his cursing book.

66 Scottish Calvinism is, for most, a frame of mind rather than a religious dogma. 99

The next largest denomination is the Roman Catholic church, which was never quite wiped out by the Kirk in its glory days and was greatly enlarged by floods of Irish immigrants, fleeing Ireland's famines. (Exchanges of population between Scotland and Ireland are partly responsible for the religious hostility that plagues Northern Ireland and is also to be seen in certain elements of life in Scotland.) The recent huge immigration of Poles to Scotland has caused the Catholic churches to burst at the seams, and priests have been sent for from Poland to care for their flocks.

Scottish Calvinism is, for most, a frame of mind rather than a religious dogma, but it does not get a good press, being associated with intolerance, joyless-ness, fatalism and a sanctimonious 'I'm better than you' attitude. Its essential teachings were once summed up as:

> 'You can and you can't,
> You will and you won't;
> You'll be damned if you do
> And damned if you don't.'

Although very small in number, extreme Presbyterian sects remain, particularly in remote country and island districts. Their pronouncements attract news coverage, not because their views are widely shared, but because they are now so different from the easy-going norm. Yet Calvinism is still deeply ingrained in the Scottish soul. A poet told of how, overcome by the joy of sunshine and blue sky, he cried out what a fine day it was. The woman to whom he spoke replied, "We'll pay for it, we'll pay for it."

66 Every Scottish child knows the question 'How is he (or she) getting on?' To fail to get on is a cardinal sin. **99**

Getting on

Every Scottish child knows the question – addressed over its head to its parents – "How is she (or he) getting on?" This means is he or she being successful, and it doesn't end with schooldays but will still be asked when the child goes to college or embarks on a career. To fail to get on is a cardinal sin. The person asking the question invariably has a story ready about their own Jean or Sandy, who is of course getting on just fine, top of the class, graduating with honours or joining the board of an international company.

'Getting on' is a national aspiration. One small boy regularly assured his parents that he was getting on fine and he was top of his class. One day they happened to ask how many were in the class, and his answer was: "Oh, just me and another wee laddie."

Class distinctions

Measuring themselves, as they so often do, against the English, the Scots like to believe that they are a relatively classless society. It is one of their best-loved myths. A Writer to the Signet (a superior kind of solicitor) who has been to one of Scotland's great endowed schools and is a member of several exclusive clubs, such as the Honourable Company of Edinburgh Golfers, with its years-long waiting list, is unlikely to feel he is in the same social class as an unemployed construction worker just because they bear the same surname.

> **66** The aristocracy have adjusted to a society in which football players and pop singers enjoy more prestige than they do. **99**

Class is more an economic matter than a social one. Scotland is undoubtedly an open society. Otherwise 'getting on' would be far less possible. A much-loved tale is of a visitor to the Highlands who meets an old man digging the fields of his croft all by himself and asks what his children are doing. "Ach, well, one of them is a judge in what they call the High Court, and one of them is a professor of medicine at Oxford University. But the youngest has done very well – he's the minister of the next parish."

The Scottish aristocracy are alive and kicking, and many of them live comfortably in their castles and country houses, but

> **66 The pragmatic streak in the Scottish character assures them that what goes up must come down again. 99**

they no longer dominate the scene. A high proportion of the landscape is still owned by them – something the ordinary Scot resents. But many estates are now in the hands of foreigners, whom they resent less. The aristocracy in turn have adjusted to a society in which football players and pop singers enjoy more prestige than they do.

Dog in the manger

The Scots have their full share of that strange human satisfaction in seeing a high-flyer brought low. Nemesis is never very far away in Scotland. The pragmatic streak in the Scottish character assures them that what goes up must come down again.

It is good to get on, but right to be modest about it – after all, success may not last. The classic Scottish put-down is not based on social status; it comes from perceiving an opportunity to puncture a balloon. This is irresistible to the Scottish mind. Robert Burns happened to be present when a sailor rescued a well-to-do merchant who had fallen into Greenock harbour. When the man offered his rescuer a shilling, the onlookers protested at such meanness. Burns intervened, and said, "The gentleman best knows himself the value of his own life."

> **66** Thriftiness is a national habit. When Scots have money, they don't flaunt it. They save it. **99**

Thrift

Ostentatious display of wealth is frowned on in Scotland, though people do get away with it, especially if they are 'characters'. When they have money, the Scots don't flaunt it. They save it. Thriftiness is a national habit. It was a Scottish minister who started the world's first savings bank for his parishioners.

Not so long ago Scottish meanness was a regular music-hall joke. 'Two taxis collide in Aberdeen; twenty passengers killed.' For this, the English must be thanked. The Scots were always poor, always had to

24

count their pennies carefully. Their wealthier neighbours could not help noticing, and making humorous comments. To the Scots themselves, there was nothing funny about it. Money was and is a serious matter. It is no coincidence that a Scotsman started the Bank of England; or that Edinburgh should today be Europe's third most important financial centre (after Frankfurt and London).

Thrift should not be confused with meanness, of which the Scots do not approve. A Scotsman sitting down to breakfast at a guesthouse and, eyeing the modest dod of honey given him for his toast, addressed the proprietor with the comment: "I see you keep a bee."

Behaviour

A nation of non-conformists

The Scots are not a particularly conformist nation – a result, perhaps, of their firmly held opinions. With their strong sense of community, local and national, they are generally law-abiding, as long as the laws make sense to them. Any hint of exploitation raises their hackles, and they have a great dislike of officious people who take it on themselves to tell others what to do. Such folk are liable to be put down with remarks like, "Does your mother ken you're out?"

Scots are quite good at queuing, if only to make sure that nobody steals a march on them, but they are not the sort of people to wait patiently for the green light to appear at a road crossing if they can see there is no traffic coming.

Those responsible for attracting foreign companies to invest in Scotland make much of the 'Protestant work ethic' which is supposed to guarantee a dedicated and docile work force. In fact the Scots, though not averse to hard work, are far from docile as a work force.

66 When you reach the West Highlands, time ceases to have its familiar meaning. 99

In most activities they are unhurried. People will stop and gossip in the street. Shop assistants will chat to customers, even when people are waiting to be served. This is true even in the big cities, and when you reach the West Highlands, time ceases to have its familiar meaning. The ceilidh (shindig) advertised for 9 o'clock in the village hall may start getting under way by 11 pm. On the island of Mull, they say "There are no half-hours", and on the Isle of Eigg, asked when the ferry boat was due, a local replied: "Weel, she'll be coming sometimes sooner, and whiles (at other times) earlier, and sometimes before that again."

The Scots set store by good public behaviour, perhaps because most of them live in towns and cities, often in apartment blocks known as tenements, with shared responsibilities for keeping the public areas clean and tidy. It is a land of neat front gardens, scrubbed doorsteps and polished front doors. Round the back may be a tip of empty bottles and abandoned fridges, but round the back is out of sight.

The family

The majority of Scottish mothers have a job, even if it's only part-time. As a result, the cohesion of the once mother-centred family life has suffered.

Mothers remain the chief influence on their children, in charge of all day-by-day activity and of the household budget. Father traditionally brought home his pay-packet, was given some of it back, and repaired to the pub. He would no more have thought of helping

> **Many Scotsmen still regard 'women's work' as beneath their dignity.**

with the cooking or housework than walking naked along Princes Street. This attitude survives, and many Scotsmen still regard 'women's work' as beneath their dignity.

In an uncomfortably close-to-home joke, a Scottish couple win a million pounds on the National Lottery. "At last," says the wife, "I won't have to sweep the stairs with that old broom any more." "Of course not, hen," replies her husband. "Now I can afford to get you a new one."

The Scots emotional reticence does not apply to family. Families are quite close-knit and family feeling is strong. In cities, many young adults continue to live in the parental home while working or studying, instead of opting for an independent lifestyle in a flat.

The elderly are far from being a forgotten or isolated part of society. An important factor in family life is Granny, who often lives quite near her grown-up children, perhaps only one or two streets away, and plays a big part in the lives of her grandchildren, giving them their 'tea' (early evening meal) and taking them to the park. This role is good both for the children and for Granny herself, who features prominently in many children's playground songs, like 'Ye canna shove yir Granny aff a bus'.

> **66 Granny features prominently in many children's playground songs, like 'Ye canna shove yir Granny aff a bus'. 99**

Conversation & Gestures

Taxonomists by nature, the Scots like to classify you. After an initial inspection, they will ask you questions, designed to elicit, more or less discreetly, what sort of person you are. Once they have filed you appropriately, they will talk about other things.

As a people they can be quite formal, and the easy,

almost instant use of a first name, so common in England and America, is less frequent. At the same time, a lady on a Glasgow bus is likely to be addressed by the driver as 'hen': "Will ye move up, hen, and make room for the rest of them?" And if you get a seat, your neighbour, after the routine swift inspection, is quite likely to start a conversation, if only to say "It's awfully cold today."

There are two gestures often seen during Scots conversation. One is to separate the two hands as widely as possible. This is to demonstrate the size of the fish that the speaker almost caught. The other is to bring forefinger and thumb so close together they almost touch. This is to illustrate how close the speaker's golf ball got to the hole without going in.

> **It can be hard work conversing with a Scot. They are often alarmingly well-informed, and the more remote the community, the truer this is likely to be.**

Apart from essential exchanges about the weather, it can be hard work conversing with a Scot. But don't mistake taciturnity for lack of interest. As with many people who are quite slow to start a conversation, it can be difficult to get a Scot in full flow to stop. They are often alarmingly well-informed, and the more remote the community, the truer this is likely to be.

The secret of how to get a conversation going is either to display ignorance, or to initiate a debate.

The former is safer, the second is altogether more lively. Express a firm opinion on any subject from global warming to driving standards and your Scottish friend will seize on it like a terrier, shake it around, and convince you that you are utterly mistaken.

❝ Express a firm opinion and your Scottish friend will seize on it like a terrier, shake it around, and convince you that you are utterly mistaken. ❞

Once a conversation is well under way, and a good argument is being had, the jabbing forefinger comes into play. Scots often like to make a point as forcibly as possible, and can quickly become exasperated if it does not seem to be getting home. It can be safest in the end just to agree.

As an idea develops, it can lead down strange paths. Scepticism is often taken about as far as it can go. It was David Hume, the country's most celebrated philosopher who demonstrated the national talent for taking a point of view to a stage where it is unprovable either way, of absolutely no practical use, but mentally highly satisfying. There is an abstract and intellectual quality to the Scots mind that rejoices in uncomfortable thoughts. A true Scot would sooner be right than rich, any time.

❝ There is an abstract and intellectual quality to the Scots mind. A true Scot would sooner be right than rich, any time. ❞

Greetings and toasts

For the stranger, the most baffling of the greetings the Scots exchange with one another is this:

First Scot: "Aye aye."
Second Scot: "Aye."

Short though it is, 'Aye' can be rich in meaning, depending on the use of inflection, position of the eyebrows, and movement, if any, of the lips. It can communicate anything from 'Not you again', to 'How nice to see you'. (It is possible that it is also the origin of the American greeting 'Hi'.)

The Scots have ritual exchanges. When offering someone the national drink, a Scot will not say, "Would you like a whisky?" but "Will you take a dram?" To which the proper answer is "Oh, just a sensation". This means, yes please, a big one. If you don't want a big one, the correct response is "Oh, just a wee sensation".

Matters are not over once your glass is in your hand. Your host raises his and utters the words: "*Slainte mhath*." This is Gaelic for 'Good health' (pronounced more or less 'slanjah-vah') and is about as much Gaelic as the majority of Scots know. The correct response is "*Slainte mhór*" (pronounced 'slan-

> **"** 'Aye' can be rich in meaning, depending on the use of inflection, position of the eyebrows, and movement, if any, of the lips. **"**

31

jah-vore'), which means 'Great health'. Salutations may end at this point and quaffing begin, or the host may go one further and cap his guest with "*Sláinte gu síorraidh*" ('slan-jah-ga-shorrah'), which means 'Health for ever'. After that the serious drinking can really begin.

Sense of Humour

It is easy to know when a Scot is telling you something funny. The face assumes an extra solemnity; the voice becomes drier; the tone more sepulchral. Like other emotional signals, humour is kept under tight covers.

66 **When a Scot is telling you something funny, the face assumes an extra solemnity, the voice becomes drier, the tone more sepulchral.** 99

There is no nonsense or fantasy in Scottish humour. There is always a point, and frequently a moral. It has an earthy streak, like the tale of the country tramp who specialised in begging from farmhouses. Picking up a dried-up cow-turd, he would knock at the door and request some dry bread to make 'a piece' (a sandwich) of it. The farmers' wives would always tell him to throw it away and give him a decent 'piece'. One day, however, he encountered the farmer at home. The farmer was just as horrified as his wife would have been: "Man, you can't eat that," he said. "Throw it away. Come round to the cow-shed with me and I'll find you a nice, fresh, hot one."

There is often more than a hint of salt-over-the-shoulder superstition involved. The Scots frequently make jokes about the things they fear, like old age or death, as in the tale of Old MacPherson. To celebrate his 95th birthday, his cronies sent round an attractive young 'masseuse'. When he opened the door, she said brightly, "I'm here to give you super sex." He ruminated on this for a while, then finally said, "I'll have the soup."

Though the Scots like a joke to have a point, the point, ideally, should not be too obvious. They relish above all the moment between the end of the joke and the laugh (or at any rate the grimace) of the person to whom it is told, when the humour finally sinks in.

> **Although the Scots like a joke to have a point, the point should not be too obvious.**

Their own idiosyncrasies will often be targets for mockery. It was a Scottish playwright, W. Gordon Smith, who made one of the characters in his play, Mister Jock, say: "Son, I've been round the world, and Scotland is the only country where six and half a dozen are never the same thing."

No single place in Scotland is a butt for the humour of everyone else. The closest to an exception is Aberdeen, which has somehow acquired a reputation for excessive Scottish thriftiness. For example:

If a Scotsman opens his purse, the moths fly out.
If an Aberdonian opens his purse, the moths are all dead.

While the wits of Glasgow may sometimes mock the slow-thinking countryman, Scottish jokes are mainly made at the expense of outsiders, especially outsiders who seem too pleased with themselves, as in the following anecdote:

> An Australian came into an Edinburgh bar and stood happily chatting for a time, before one of the regulars asked him, "Where are you from, pal?" "I'm from the finest country in the whole wide world," said the Aussie. "Is that so?" said the local. "You have a damn funny accent for a Scotsman."

A rich seam of Scots humour is mined from cynicism, exemplified by this remark about some dead Scotsman who had lived to a great old age: "He got real pleasure from the fact that he had lived so long that he was more time getting the pension than he had actually worked for it."

66 A rich seam of Scots humour is mined from cynicism. 99

From the hard edge of Scotland's urban culture comes a distinctive form of humour, personified in the life of 'Rab C. Nesbitt', a sitcom that ran for more than a decade. Nesbitt was an archetypal Glaswegian layabout with a paunch protruding from his string vest, unemployed, boozy, work-shy, male chauvinist to the nth degree, but always ready with a wisecrack such as, "There's nothing that restores yer faith more in human nature than meeting some poor bastard that's just as mad as yourself."

> **66 Until comparatively recently, Scottish catering was something to be feared. 99**

Other Scottish comedians, like Robbie Coltrane and Billy Connolly, have tapped this fruitful vein, as in Connolly's tale of the man who killed his wife and buried her in the back garden. He showed the grave to his friend, who said, "What did you leave her bum sticking out for?" And the man said, "I need somewhere to park my bike."

Eating & Drinking

Food

Scotland is not one of the great culinary centres of the world. Until comparatively recently, Scottish catering was something to be feared; visitors came despite the food. Things have improved since the 18th century when a visitor to an Edinburgh chop-house observed that the cook was so filthy, that if you threw him against the wall, he would have stuck to it.

The Scots have learned to exploit their own distinctive traditions in this area as in all others. An array of local specialities beckons from the menus – porridge and kippers at breakfast, soups like 'cullen skink' and 'cock-a-leekie', curious vegetable combinations like 'clapshot', basically mashed 'neeps' (swede) and potatoes, and 'stovies' (meat and potato stew). But there is no cause for alarm. Essentially, Scotland excels in good plain fare – fresh fish, smoked salmon, roast beef, potatoes. The Scots firmly believe they grow the world's best potatoes. There is rumoured to be a hotel in the north-east that has a potato list as well as a wine list; you select your preference from among the many varieties: Kerr's Pink, Catriona, Shaft's Express, Sutton's Abundance, Maris Piper, Duke of York (both White and Red) – the waiter will advise if necessary.

> **It has been said that the use of the paunch of the animal gives 'the touch of romantic barbarism so dear to the Scottish heart'.**

The haggis was probably imported to Scotland a thousand years ago by the Vikings. It suits a frugal nation whose sheep population numbers about the same as the human population. Traditionally encased in a sheep's stomach, and boiled in a pot, haggis is a pudding of minced-up mutton remnants and offal, with oatmeal, onions and spices. It has been said that the use of the paunch of the animal gives 'the touch of romantic barbarism so dear to the Scottish heart'. In fact, it is a very tasty dish, and many countries have something similar – it took the Scots to turn it into a tradition.

The Scots do eat their traditional dishes, but almost always at home. When they go out to eat, they become international, and head for a Chinese or Indian or Mexican or Turkish restaurant. They are also a great people for take-aways, known as 'cairry-oots'. The fish and chip shop is highly popular, and its range usually extends to oriental food as well as such uniquely Scottish delicacies as haggis in batter and the deep-fried Mars Bar.

Perhaps the cold, damp winters and long, dark nights have something to do with it, but the Scots are one of the most sweet-toothed peoples on earth. They eat more sweet biscuits and cakes per head of the population than any other nation.

> **They eat more sweet biscuits and cakes per head of the population than any other nation.**

In Scotland you will find a whole range of sweet products and bakery items that are unknown elsewhere in the world. There are baps, floury rolls, oatcakes, butteries (a kind of croissant), scones, shortbreads, and a variety of pastries, including the Scotch pie – a savoury mutton pie, often sold at half-time at football matches; and the Forfar bridie – a monster handful of pastry, shaped rather like a Cornish pasty, packed with meat, vegetables and gravy.

The main family meal of 'high tea' is served at any time between 5 o'clock and 7 o'clock. It consists of a cooked first course, accompanied by bread and butter, and followed by a formidable array of scones, buns, cake and sugar-sprinkled shortbread, all washed down with copious quantities of well-sugared tea.

Drink

As many people have noted, the Scots are partial to their 'bevvy'. Only confectionery is more widely on sale than alcohol, and pubs are open throughout the day. The Scottish pub, once a cheerless, sawdust-floored, guilt-inducing place, is nowadays quite pleasant and may even have tables and seats.

> **The Scots are partial to their 'bevvy'. Only confectionery is more widely on sale than alcohol.**

Whisky is a great source of discussion and argument among the Scots. Two eminent scholars once fell into ferocious dispute, one claiming that the other had said two shocking things – first, that whisky was brought to Scotland from Ireland; second, that the Irish had used it as an embrocation for sick mules and it took the Scots to apply it to internal consumption.

For dedicated whisky drinkers talk centres on 'single malt' whiskies, and whether those from the heathery glens of the east are superior to those from the salt-sprayed coasts of the west, or vice versa. Both have their devotees, and a good Scottish host will make sure that he has a supply of each, plus perhaps one from Orkney and another from one of the Highland distilleries. Each brand has its own aroma and its own 'tradition', lovingly elaborated upon by generations of public relations consultants.

Inevitably, a mystique has grown, or been cultivated, around malt whisky. The Scots, who will cheerfully pour a hefty slug of lemonade into a glass of blended whisky, are apt to put on a face of solemn horror if you 'adulterate' malt in the same way. Some say that malts should be drunk neat. Others insist that the addition of a little water brings out the aroma and flavour.

> **❝ Whisky is by far Scotland's biggest export, despite determined efforts by many Scots to consume the whole output. ❞**

The maturing stocks of Scotch whisky are said to be more valuable than the bullion in the Bank of England. Whisky is by far Scotland's biggest export, despite determined efforts by many Scots to consume the whole output.

Scottish beer is a puzzle to an incomer. There is a range of oddly named dark ales – eighty shilling (80/-), sixty shilling (60/-), and small, menacing bottles containing a brew known as a 'wee heavy'. These beers can be drunk on their own, but their true function is to be a chaser to whisky. Many pub drinkers have in front of them two glasses from which they drink alternately, a large one of beer and a small one of whisky. This is called 'a-half-and-half', and outside some heavy-duty brews found in Poland and South America, it is one of the most lethal mixtures known to man.

> **Small, menacing bottles containing beer can be drunk on their own, but their true function is to be a chaser to whisky.**

A small quirk that underlines Scotland's distinctness is that it is the only country in the West where Coca-Cola is not the most popular soft drink. The Scots go instead for a bright orange local product called 'Irn Bru' (pronounced Iron Brew), whose advertising slogan is 'made from girders'.

Health & Hygiene

Well entrenched in the Scottish persona is the belief that the Scots are a hardy lot, immune to the ailments that afflict weaker nations. Statistics tend to contradict this. In reality, according to one speaker (though he was exaggerating for effect): "The typical Scot has bad teeth, a good chance of cancer, a liver under severe stress and a heart attack pending." Certainly, the Scots' love of sweet things doesn't do their teeth any good – it's a country where dentists do splendidly.

A very high number of Scots fall victim to heart attacks. A Glasgow golf club has become the first non-medical institution to install a defibrillator machine, to revive sufferers from heart failure. And, in a country that produces one of the world's most popular spirituous drinks, it is no surprise that alcoholism is a problem. Average life expectancy for the Scot is still two years less than it is for the English and Welsh.

However, if you have to be ill, Scotland is a good place to be ill in. It has a long tradition of medical education and expertise. The Scots were pioneers in anatomy, anaesthetics

❝ If you have to be ill, Scotland is a good place to be ill in. It has a long tradition of medical education and expertise. ❞

and gynaecology, and these days are in the forefront of research in genetics, cancer and (happily for the nation) heart disease. They have excellent hospitals and produce numerous doctors, not all of whom are exported.

The national interest in the workings of the mind has prompted many Scots to become psychologists and psychiatrists. It was a Scottish 'shrink' who, applying a typically Scottish thought-process to his subject, came up with the concept that 'madness may not just be breakdown. It may also be breakthrough'. In his view, you'd be mad not to be mad.

Cleanliness

Hygiene is something of an issue in Scotland. In the old days, it used to play a secondary role to the need to keep warm. Many a Scottish child used to be sewn into its winter underwear in November and wasn't unpicked until March.

Today, most people have central heating and modern bathrooms, in which the bath, rather than the shower, is the centrepiece – they like a good wallow. But old habits die hard: while the majority bathe or shower every day, a sizeable proportion still clings to the idea that once a week is quite enough.

Custom & Tradition

In a world where people increasingly dress the same, eat other nations' foods, forget their own folklore and travel the globe to see reconstructed versions of other peoples' customs, the Scots hold several trump cards.

66 The bagpipe was defined by one critic as 'the missing link between music and noise'. 99

They maintain the bagpipe, an instrument largely abandoned by the rest of Europe in the 14th century, and defined by one critic as 'the missing link between music and noise'. They have strathspeys and reels (traditional dances) which add to the gaiety of festive occasions, along with a distinctive national costume worn by men and boys. They have ritual gatherings known as Highland Games, with piping and dancing competitions, and at which feats of strength such as tossing the caber are practised (not so long ago it was wrenching the legs off a newly slaughtered cow).

To all this, add golf, salmon fishing, deer stalking, grouse shooting – each one an activity ingrained with its own lore and tradition. Top it off with the exploits of such historic figures as William Wallace, Robert the Bruce, and Bonnie Prince Charlie, and you have a tourist executive's dream: Theme Park Scotland.

> 66 They have ritual gatherings with piping and dancing competitions, and at which feats of strength such as tossing the caber are practised – not so long ago it was wrenching the legs off a newly slaughtered cow. 99

The surprising thing is that, to a large extent, it is real. The Scots go to their offices and factories, schools and shops, wearing the same chain-store clothes as every other nation. You may not see the kilt worn that much in the street, but go to a wedding, a ball, a university graduation or an international rugby match, and you will see any number of kilts with, exposed between the kilt and the thick woolly socks, perhaps an inch or two of the wearer's pale, hairy knees.

At parties and dances people leap to their feet for

Scottish dancing. Most can manage the simpler dances, like 'Strip the Willow' and 'The Gay Gordons', the men lumbering gallantly into action, steered by the women who are better at it (the macho tradition of school playgrounds having made boys chary of going to dancing classes). For the more complicated reels, the band usually provides a caller, but the hardest ones, like the 'Reel of the 51st Highland Division', are best left to those who really know their intricacies.

> **The macho tradition of school playgrounds made boys chary of going to Scottish dancing classes.**

Even the Highland Games, which are hugely appreciated by visitors, would not survive if they were not also enjoyed and supported by the local communities. The Scots have the splendid luxury of being able to play at being Scottish as well as actually being Scottish.

Clans

Clans are another part of the game of being Scottish that the Scots so much enjoy. The word clan originally meant 'children', meaning the descendants of a single person, and each clan claims descent from a single Adam-like ancestor. In the case of some clans, it is Adam himself. When a Macleod and a MacLean were disputing the age of their respective clans, Macleod said, "We never saw you on board Noah's ark." To which Maclean replied: "Who ever heard of a MacLean that didn't have his own boat?"

Once upon a time, the clansmen would obey the war signal of the Fiery Cross, take their 'claymores', or broadswords, from their hiding place in the thatch and follow their chief into battle. Nowadays, although there is a Standing Conference of Clan Chiefs, the chieftains have no authority of any sort. Many have formed Clan Associations, and some of the larger ones, like the MacDonalds and the Campbells, have a well-organised international network with regular newsletters, web sites and gatherings. They are harmless, indeed socially valuable organisations, far removed, in the case of such clans as the MacGregors and Robertsons, from their warlike forebears who used to go cattle-raiding far afield, terrorising farmers and villagers. But these old stories of derring-do still put a swing in the modern clansman's kilt.

> **Each clan claims descent from a single ancestor. In the case of some clans, it is Adam himself.**

Tribalism

Before there were clans in Scotland and spanning a much longer period, there were tribes. The clans, in fact, represent a partial survival of the ancient tribal organisation. In the behaviour and character of modern Scots, the remnants of tribal attitudes still colour much of their views and lives. This can be seen in their attachment to the land itself, especially their own area of it, in their clannishness, in their fondness for tradition and small rituals, in their long historic memories, and their competitive spirit.

> **66 Much of the jigsaw of Scottish character falls into place when you bear in mind that the Scot is still, quite unconsciously, a tribesman or woman at heart. 99**

Much of the jigsaw of Scottish character falls into place when you bear in mind that the Scot is still, quite unconsciously, a tribesman or woman at heart.

Kilts and tartans

In ancient times Highlanders wore kilts (whose Gaelic name means 'little wrap') and plaids ('big wrap'), which were dyed using natural dyes, and woven in the Highlands. They were usually of striped or checked design known as tartan, but not of any single or defining pattern. In battle, clansmen threw off their plaids and fought in their shirts.

Tartan (from the French tiretaine which was a wool/linen mixture) has been in existence for thousands of years. Some intriguing archaeological finds of woven cloth in eastern Europe and the Far East show just how far back in time checked cloth existed. However, today's plethora of brightly coloured tartans dates from the 19th-century surge of romantic interest in Scotland and the Highlands that was vastly encouraged by Queen Victoria's visits to her castle of Balmoral (which she carpeted in tartan, of course).

Not slow to spot an excellent marketing opportunity, the tailors of Edinburgh commissioned tartans for every clan name, and sold them to a public all too ready to believe that they were the real thing. Thousands of different tartans have been devised: according to one authority, there are 58 for 'Stewart' alone.

> **❝ When a Scotsman wears his kilt he acquires an extra swagger: he has become a colourful figure. ❞**

There are craggy Highland lairds who hold that one should never wear the kilt outside the Highlands. There are those who say you should only wear it if you can prove your connection to the clan whose tartan you are wearing. But the genial folk who run Highland-dress shops cut briskly through all this flim-flam. They have name charts to show that just about everyone is connected to a Scottish Highland clan.

When a Scotsman wears his kilt, whether he is at a society wedding or is one of the Tartan Army – the name given to the fans that follow the nation's football team – he acquires an extra swagger: he has become a colourful figure, with a skean dhu (dagger) in his stocking and money in his sporran, and he plays up to it with the enthusiasm suggested by the joke:

Queen Victoria: "Is anything worn beneath the kilt?"

Highlander: "No, ma'am, it's all in working order."

'Auld Lang Syne'

Scots link hands at the end of an evening's celebration to sing this traditional song by Robert Burns. Translated from Scots to English, the title would be 'Days of Long Ago'; but its magic would be lost. Like all tribal chants, the sense of the words is less important than the feeling of togetherness they create. The fact that it's all but incomprehensible is by the way.

Hogmanay

The Scots have taken out a patent on New Year's Eve, called it Hogmanay, and achieved the astonishing feat of making dark and icy Edinburgh an international tourist magnet in mid-winter. The old Northern festival of Yule was never forgotten in Scotland. It was an important point in the calendar, marking the middle of winter. With the days at their darkest and the nights at their longest – it was a wonderful excuse for a party.

> **The Scots have taken out a patent on New Year's Eve, and called it Hogmanay.**

Its pagan associations have all but been forgotten, but the party has got bigger. Whisky, bagpipes, 'Auld Lang Syne', and Black Bun (a New Year cake described by Robert Louis Stevenson as 'a dense black substance, inimical to life') combine to make it special. In many places the revelry has moved from the firelit hearths of people's homes to the bonfires and fireworks of public parks, with gatherings numbered in tens of thousands.

> **Like all tribal chants, the sense of the words is less important than the feeling of togetherness.**

As a result, the ancient custom of 'first-footing' (being first across the threshold after the midnight bells have rung) has gone into a decline, except in the smaller towns and villages, where partying from house to house still goes on into the early hours. Even there, though, not many Scotsmen nowadays set off to their neighbour's carrying a lump of coal and wisp of straw intended to ensure warmth and prosperity in the new year ahead.

Burns nights

Burns Nights are one of the rituals of Scottish life which the Scots themselves often mock, but their popularity shows no sign of dying out, so a visitor gets an excellent opportunity to see his hosts celebrating their Scottishness with great intensity and alarming enthusiasm. On 25th January (Robert Burns's birthday), hundreds of thousands of Scots throughout the world sit down to a supper in his honour. A highly ritualised event, it involves a piper preceding the cook who bears a dish of haggis, the recital of Burns's poem Address to a Haggis and the ceremonious dirking (cutting open) of the haggis. Only then are the guests actually permitted to consume it.

> **❝ Diners follow the speech with intense interest: each table has organised a sweep on the time it will last. ❞**

After the meal, there is a toast to the Immortal Memory of Burns himself. This is, in fact, a speech which diners follow with intense interest, perhaps because of their deep familiarity with the poet's works, but more likely because each table has organised a sweep on its length. (The speech is not necessarily literary: at a Burns Night organised by doctors, the main speaker gave a diagnosis of what Burns died of.) Other 'toasts' to 'The Lassies' and the 'Reply to the Lassies' follow, along with recitations of Burns's poems and the singing of Burns's songs. Burns having been a notable drinker, many emulate him as a further tribute.

Nessie

An ancient legend tells how, in the 6th century, St. Columba met a monster in the River Ness and sent it packing. He was so successful that nothing more was heard of it until the 1930s, when there was a rash of claimed 'sightings' which have continued ever since.

Several books have been written on Nessie and

many investigations made – all inconclusive. Just because a monster is not found, say the believers, does not mean it does not exist. Meanwhile, the local economy has benefited enormously from monster-spotters. Many local people genuinely believe there is 'something' in Loch Ness. Others are equally convinced that

> ❝ Just because a monster has not been found does not mean it does not exist. ❞

it is all humbug. However, unless the loch, which covers 20 miles and is 600 feet deep, is emptied, Nessie will live on.

Obsessions

Themselves

One of the first things that the visitor realises is that the Scots are quite obsessively Scottish. It is not just that they are different and they want you to notice it, it is that Scottishness itself is a burning issue. Enter any bookshop in Scotland and you will be faced with a massive selection of books on all things Scottish: these are not just there for the visitors. Should you

> ❝ One of the first things that the visitor realises is that the Scots are quite obsessively Scottish. ❞

happen to observe that Scotland has no famous composer, they will recall that Norway's greatest composer, Grieg, was the grandson of a Scottish emigrant.

The Scots know who they are, but they don't know what they are. In the days when they ran the British Empire for the English, this didn't matter, but now the empire is gone and Scotland's southern neighbour is once again Little England, many Scots are wondering furiously what their purpose is. No-one has yet come up with an answer, but the existence of the problem ensures that Scots maintain their serious expressions.

Scots, Scotch and Scottish

Three adjectives define 'of Scotland':

- 'Scots' is used for things that have to do with culture, especially language, or that are in some way typical of the nation; for example, 'he talks with a good Scots burr', or 'she's a braw Scots lass'.
- 'Scotch', once the everyday adjective for describing 'of Scotland', began to get a bad name for itself because it was used by the English in so many denigratory expressions, and it fell into disuse. It survives in terms like Scotch whisky and Scotch broth, and could be said to be making something of a comeback. But it has a long way to go.
- 'Scottish' is now the standard adjective. Thus, a Scots poem is a poem written in Scots, but a Scottish poem is a poem written by a Scot or about Scotland.

The three words need careful handling.

The news

The Scots are voracious consumers of newsprint. At least eight morning and evening newspapers are published in Scotland, as well as four Sunday ones, all in addition to the 'national' British newspapers, many of which have a special Scottish edition. The latter is a point of pride: one publicity poster claimed:

'*Sunday Times Scotland* – The English just don't get it.'

Scotland has its own branch of the BBC (always under pressure for not broadcasting enough Scottish news). There are two independent television stations – STV, which covers central and northern Scotland, and Border Television for the south of the country; and a new BBC Alba, a Gaelic language digital television channel, as yet unavailable to most of the highland and island audience for which it is intended because they do not have access to it.

The Scots love to read about themselves, and every community has at least one weekly newspaper where local news takes priority. The apocryphal tale of the Aberdeen newspaper which in 1912 published the headline, 'Aberdeen Man Drowned in Atlantic. Titanic Sinks' may not be true in fact, but it certainly is in spirit.

> **The tale of the newspaper that published the headline, '*Aberdeen Man Drowned in Atlantic. Titanic Sinks*' may not be true in fact, but it is in spirit.**

The weather

It's a good idea to have a comment on the weather ready, in case you talk to someone, or someone talks to you. The weather is a constant topic of conversation, which is remarkable given that Scotland only offers two main types of weather, wet or dry, with the sub-attributes of windy or not windy. However, the permutations offered by these conditions are quite enough for meaningful communication.

> **The weather is a constant topic of conversation, which is remarkable given that Scotland only offers two main types of weather, wet or dry.**

A visitor may make the opening gambit: "A bit wet today", to which the reply may be, "Aye, but not so windy." Or you may choose to start with the wind, or lack of it: "It's a nice, fresh breeze", to which the reply may be, "Aye, a grand day." On days when it is both wet and windy, people just look at one another from under their rain-hats, and say: "Oh, my!"

Fine rain, or a steady drizzle, is referred to as 'Scotch mist' and a well-known piece of weather lore runs: 'If you can't see Ben Nevis, it means it's raining. If you can see Ben Nevis, it means it's about to rain.'

Football

One of the reasons the Scots are so keen on the news is to keep up with events in Scottish football. Among

Europeans, the Scots watch more club football matches than any other country except Albania.

On Saturdays, still the day when most football matches are played, you can detect a different tone in the newsreader's voice. International items of the deepest import are hurried through with scant regard. The nation is waiting for the real news – the results of the Scottish Football League.

As a founder of the international game, the Scots have managed to be treated as a real national side despite not

> **A local definition of an atheist is someone who supports neither Rangers nor Celtic.**

being an independent nation. Scotland has a full pattern of national soccer, from the Premier League down to the Third Division. Scottish football is a tribal business, with fierce local loyalties. In the case of Rangers and Celtic, two Premier League teams who confront each other in Glasgow, there is a lingering element of Protestant and Catholic rivalry, to the extent that a local definition of an atheist is someone who supports neither one team nor the other. A similar rivalry occurs in Edinburgh between Heart of Midlothian and Hibernian.

Even without this element, a local derby, as between Dundee and Dundee United, calls forth deep emotions. The football terracing is one zone where the Scots freely indulge their feelings. Football is a passion for many Scots for whom it is the national game in a way that golf is not. It was a Scottish-born football manager, Bill Shankly, who said, "Some people think football is a matter of life or death. I can tell them it's more serious than that." In the annual international with England real nationalistic fervour moves the Scottish supporters, as though the battles of Bannockburn (1314) or Flodden (1513) were being refought each time.

Leisure & Pleasure

Helped by the fact that their cities are surrounded by beautiful open countryside, the Scots take their leisure seriously. And they have a wide range of activities to choose from. What is most remarkable, in a country where winter lasts from October to April, and summer has been referred to as a weekend in July, is that nearly all their leisure activities are outdoor ones. An American wit commented that "If the Scots knew enough to stay indoors when it rained, they would never get any exercise".

Golf and games

If you want to provoke a vigorous if localised disturbance, try telling a Scot that golf originated in Holland and was introduced to Scotland by Dutch traders. The Scots have absolutely no doubt about which side of the North Sea the game began. This is the great national game for all ages and both sexes to actually play, rather than watch, and in Scotland, where every village has a golf course, it need not be expensive.

There are 11 golf courses at St. Andrews, where the mandarins of the Royal and Ancient Golf Club (or R&A) maintain golf's world headquarters. The celebrated Old Course can be hard to get on to, but impecunious students at the town's universityare rumoured to get up at 5 o'clock in the morning and get in a free round before the greenkeepers have had breakfast.

> **"Students at St. Andrews university are rumoured to get up at 5 o'clock in the morning to get in a free round."**

In the Borders, rugby is the game, and the farmers and millworkers of this region have provided many of the players for the Scottish international side, which has won its fair share of Grand Slams against the other rugby nations.

Another popular Scottish sport is curling, akin to bowls but played by sending heavy granite stones scudding across the ice. Known as 'the roaring game', it is now enjoyed year-round on indoor rinks where the ice is more reliable.

In the Highlands they have a wild stick-and-ball game called shinty, which is similar to Irish hurling but a bit less restrained. Players have been known to scrape their opponents' eyebrows off their shinty sticks after a particularly close-fought tackle.

> **66 Novelist Eric Linklater said the only thing he had against golf was that it took you so far from the clubhouse. 99**

Central to all these activities is the club and the clubhouse. (Indeed, novelist Eric Linklater said the only thing he had against golf was that it took you so far from the clubhouse.) Scottish sportsmen are a clubbish lot. They enjoy discussing their sport over a beer or a whisky in the club bar; some, arguing comfortably over who did what in some famous competition, never get beyond it.

Skiing and climbing

The Scots do their best to pretend that their mountains are skiable in winter, even if it involves bumping over squashy remnants of snow with grassy tufts poking through. After all, it's much nearer and sometimes cheaper than going to the Alps.

But what the mountains undoubtedly offer is magnificent rock climbing and hill walking. Scottish peaks are classified as either a 'Munro' (3,000 feet plus) or a 'Corbett' (2,500 feet plus), and though anyone who goes in for 'Munro-bagging' is the subject of some mirth, it is the lifetime ambition of many to climb them all.

Scottish climbers like to perpetuate a 'hard' man or woman image, and their mountain 'bothies' (stone-built shelters) are spartan places. It is rare now to find completely new routes up the crags but there is strong competition between clubs from the different cities. Some of the finest challenges are the coastal cliffs and rock stacks, where the natural perils are increased by the fulmars that nest on the ledges and practise projectile vomiting on unsuspecting climbers.

Hunting, shooting and fishing

Another favourite pastime is fishing, preferably practised standing up to the waist in a river for several hours, or sitting in a small boat in a cloud of midges (a Scots version of the mosquito but half the size and twice as vicious).

> **Another favourite pastime is fishing, preferably practised standing up to the waist in a river for several hours, or in a small boat in a cloud of midges.**

In Scotland you can fish freely for brown trout, but if you happen to catch a salmon without having a permit, don't be surprised if a gamekeeper leaps out from behind a tree. There is a Highland saying which goes, 'A deer from the hill, a salmon from the river, and a stick from the forest is the birthright of every Gael', but many a poacher has languished in jail after trying to put this into practice.

Deer stalking and grouse and pheasant shooting are far more exclusive pursuits, requiring connections, or lots of money – but wealth is no protection from the mighty midge. Once the preserve of a landowner and his guests, bird shoots are now very often let to syndicates. Local people view these activities with an amused eye. An impartial observer remarked of an event and its participants: "They were stung by everything and everyone."

Deer stalking can involve spending the best part of a day crawling on your stomach across a mountainside through heather and sticky black bogland, with a 'gillie' (keeper) hissing angrily each time you raise your head above foliage level, only to find that the wind has changed and wafted your scent to the deer, who have moved with effortless ease to the other side of the hill.

> **66 Deer stalking can involve spending the best part of the day crawling on your stomach across the mountainside. 99**

'Gillie' literally means boy, but the gillie who accompanies you when stalking or loch-fishing is more likely to be a grizzled elder, encased in a tweed jacket and the baggy breeches known as plus-fours, economical with words, impervious to the weather and the insect life, and oozing the grittier national characteristics from every pore. When the lunch-box is opened, or the day is over, he will gravely accept a stiff dram from your flask, and may unbend so far as to utter those Scots words of praise for your day's performance: "No' bad."

Holidays

The era of mass jet travel has enabled the Scots to discover an astral object that they knew little about – the sun. In summer the Scottish population of the Canary Isles probably exceeds that of the Orkneys. It's not just the promise of unlimited sunshine and cheap wine that attracts them – it's the release of being abroad.

The responsibility of being Scottish falls from their shoulders, they become cheerful, exuberant, almost Latin in their behaviour. Often they overdo it, becoming overemotional and having to be carried back to the hotel by their friends.

> **The era of mass jet travel has enabled the Scots to discover an astral object they knew little about – the sun.**

It used to be the case that wealthy Scots went abroad and the less well-off stayed at home and went on trips on the Clyde steamers. Nowadays the wealthier ones have holiday homes in Scottish coastal villages or time-share apartments in ex-baronial castles, while the majority buy package tours to the sun.

Sex

Scotland has never made a heavy issue of marriage. Until the rest of the world caught up, it was easier both to get married and to get unmarried in Scotland than elsewhere. For a long time the sanction of the church or the registrar was not necessary in order to wed: all you needed were two witnesses – hence the large number of runaways who eloped from England to marry in the first village in Scotland, Gretna Green.

There has always been a ribald, raunchy streak somewhere in the Scottish character, which emerges in the bawdier poems of Robert Burns, but there is little romance. Romance to the Scots means the dreamy Celtic past rather than human relationships. The average Scotsman's idea of seductive language leaves a lot to be desired. A woman all dressed up for an evening out might win the compliment, 'Not bad'.

> **66 Romance to the Scots means the dreamy Celtic past rather than modern relationships. 99**

To many Scots, particularly males, sex remains a furtive affair, something that is poked fun at in this tall tale. An elderly Scot goes into a department store and asks the drapery assistant for 10 yards of apricot satin, explaining that it's to make into a nightie for his new young bride. 'But you don't need half that much,' protests the assistant. 'I ken that fine', says the old man, 'but I like a wee bit of a fumble.'

Systems

Getting about

Scotland has the shortest scheduled air-flight in the world – the two-minute trip from one Orkney isle, Westray, to its neighbour, Papa Westray. On the Isle of Barra, where the landing strip is a beach, scheduled flights have to take account not only of the times of tides, but the clearing of cattle from the sand by a local.

In outlying places, local transport, when it exists, is usually quite efficient, with post-buses carrying both passengers and the mail. Only a few of the Highlands' single track roads remain, thus removing a valuable source of conversation and complaint. On these narrow strips of asphalt, cars rocket towards each other (as if each had Jackie Stewart at the wheel) until one or other turns aside at the last moment into one of the occasional passing places. Sometimes slow drivers will actually pull into them and let you overtake – unless you have hooted and flashed your lights at them, in which case they will hunch over the steering wheel and trundle along in front of you at a steady crawl.

This is not the only hazard. Notices proclaim leaping deer, falling rocks and, more frequently, 'Unfenced

> **❝On the Isle of Barra, where the landing strip is a beach, flights have to take account not only of the times of tides, but the clearing of cattle.❞**

Road: Beware of Sheep' because sheep have a tendency to settle down on the warm tarmac to doze.

Trains in Scotland are efficient and usually run to time. But there are not very many of them. Travel by public transport, particularly on a Sunday, requires time and patience, nowhere more so than on the long single-track rail and road routes through the glens and across the moors. On a train from Kyle of Lochalsh to Glasgow, as it neared its destination and people began to assemble their belongings, a passenger was heard to remark, "Well, that's the worst of the journey over." "Where are you going?" asked his neighbour. "China," was the reply.

> **66 Sheep have a tendency to settle down on the warm tarmac of Highland roads to doze. 99**

Education

Few countries have been more adept than Scotland at managing their own mythology and keeping it up to date, due in large part to the fact that the Scots themselves believe it. This is certainly true of education, which in Scotland has always been run separately from that of the rest of the UK. Even the English are liable to say that Scottish education is best; the Scots have never doubted it. There are, of course, sceptics who say that modern educational policy in Scotland is simply the policy that obtained in England ten years ago and is now outmoded there.

Behind the screen of myth, there is real concern about the quality and style of education. Schools are less disciplined than was the case a generation ago; teachers are less respected than in the days when schoolboys were expected to salute, military-style, when passing them in the street.

Education is notionally democratic. The quality of teaching may be similar whether it is state or fee-paying, but the size of classes and the resources available are very different. Outside the cities, virtually all children go to state schools, many of which are excellent. Secondary schools in Scotland are often called academies, but any other connections with Plato would be hard to find.

> **Even the English are liable to admit that Scottish education is best; the Scots have never doubted it.**

Nearly all children are day-pupils. The few Scottish boarding schools tend to be inhabited by children of well-to-do 'Anglo-Scots', and those sent from England for the benefits of Scottish fresh air and, of course, a Scottish education.

More than half Scotland's school leavers go on to college or university, but there is concern about the 'it's not for the likes of us' attitude held by some young people. The Scottish honours degree course is a four-year one rather than the three years that applies to many courses in England. Students do not pay fees for university tuition, in contrast to their peers south of the border.

Among Scotland's 12 universities the ancient foundations still have the most prestige. St. Andrews and Edinburgh, especially, are very popular with English undergraduates, who provide almost half the annual intake, a fact that sometimes riles the Scots – although the non-Scots are charged tuition fees which tends to make up for it.

Business

Once a land of heavy industry, its central valley packed with coal mines and steelworks, with the River Clyde the world's main shipbuilding centre, Scotland has seen all that vanish well within a single lifetime. More people are now employed in service industries than in manufacturing; and women account for approximately half the workforce.

66 The Scots claim a substantial corner in information technology, and the press was quick to call the central valley 'Silicon Glen'. 99

Almost as their coal ran out, the Scots found they had some of the world's biggest offshore oil and gas deposits right on their doorstep. The country rapidly became the world centre of advanced 'offshore' technology. The costly exploitation was done by the international oil giants, who also reaped the rewards.

The Scots claim a substantial corner in information technology, and the press was quick to call the central valley 'Silicon Glen' in emulation of the California original. The on-line era has transformed the Scottish Highlands from a remote and in some ways backward area into a buzzing district of the global village.

It was Scottish emigrants who turned Hong Kong into one of the world's great trading centres, yet the Scots are not among the world's great traders. They are better known for seeing their innovations developed successfully elsewhere. Kirkpatrick Macmillan, who built the world's first effective bicycle and rode it from Dumfries to Glasgow (where he was prosecuted for causing a road accident), never pursued his invention. Henry Bell, the

> **Kirkpatrick Macmillan built the world's first effective bicycle and rode it from Dumfries to Glasgow, where he was prosecuted for causing a road accident.**

steamship pioneer, died in poverty. Another Bell, Patrick, built the first effective reaping machine, but it was eclipsed by the American McCormick's. John Logie Baird, pioneer of television, saw an alternative system to his become the standard.

There are few major enterprises still owned in Scotland by Scots. Most are partly or entirely owned elsewhere. The business cadre is managerial, acting on policy decided in Frankfurt, Seoul or Detroit. Banking and financial services are a major industry; if the Scots don't have vast amounts of wealth themselves, they certainly like looking after other people's.

Two of the traditional industries of Scotland, whisky and textiles, are sustained by the unique nature and high quality of their products and by assiduous marketing. Tweed cloth from the Hebrides and the Borders is still a basic resource for the fashion industry, though thankfully modern processing techniques no longer require the steeping of raw fabric in stale urine, which used to contribute to the distinctive aroma of the virtually indestructible Harris tweed. (It is said that you cannot throw Harris tweed away. You have to shoot it or bury it.)

> **It is said that you cannot throw Harris tweed away. You have to shoot it or bury it.**

Much energy is spent on the process of winning inward investment, that is, bribing foreign companies to set up in Scotland with huge capital grants and low rents. Empty factories and razed sites testify to the fleeting nature of such projects. But Scotland, by the size of its population and the need to provide jobs, is tied into the international game of wooing investors. The Scots play this game well, and draw on their assets whenever possible. It's not in every country that executives visiting from head office can play on a world-class golf course, or catch a salmon in a tumbling river, only a short drive from the works.

Foresters and fishermen

To the surprise of many visitors, a 'forest' in Scotland may be entirely tree-less – if it's a deer forest. But great tracts of hillside are covered in woodland, and bird and plant sanctuaries, such as the vast region of level bogland known as the 'Flow Country', are coveted by those who like to see empty landscapes populated by profitable trees. The growth of forestry as an important industry has had a mixed welcome. Serried ranks of Sitka spruce do not improve the view.

> **The growth of forestry has had a mixed welcome. Serried ranks of Sitka spruce do not improve the view.**

Hard-hit by over-fishing of the North Sea grounds and by European-imposed quotas fishing harbours now hold little more than yachts and pleasure boats. Fish farms have been established in many sea lochs. As the wild salmon becomes rarer and more expensive, the farmed variety becomes ever more plentiful. Shellfish, too, are grown like a crop. The Scots who once went out on open-decked fishing boats in oilskins and sou' westers are more likely nowadays to wear white coats and be hand-feeding a hundred thousand baby lobsters, each one in its own separate little compartment.

Farmers and crofters

The oldest business of Scotland is farming. The Aberdeen Angus bull, the Ayrshire cow, the Cheviot sheep, the Clydesdale horse, all testify to Scotland's role in the development of modern agriculture. Most urban Scots are countryfolk at heart. Older people reminisce about the October 'tattie holidays' when schools closed for two weeks and the children helped to harvest potatoes, earning enough money to pay for their new winter clothes and boots.

> **Older people reminisce about the October 'tattie holidays' when schools closed for two weeks and children helped to harvest the potatoes.**

Farmers are a close-knit community and many farms are single-family operations, with neighbours helping one another out with major tasks like harvesting and planting. It's not entirely an open-air life. All farmers have had to become experts in accountancy, if only to keep abreast of European bureaucracy and ensure that they get the maximum possible amount of subsidy. The farmer sits indoors scratching his head at his computer and calculator, while his wife is out in the fields, driving the giant-wheeled tractor.

In the Highlands and Islands, the typical agricultural unit is the croft, a tiny one-man farm. There is a whole system of grants and subsidies to support the crofters, giving rise to the definition of a croft as 'a piece of ground entirely surrounded by regulations'.

The croft being uneconomic in itself, most crofters have another job as well, such as teacher, taxi-driver, post person, or maker of Blackfaced sheep souvenirs using raw wool and pipe cleaners.

The lure of remote life has transformed some moribund West Highland communities into active places. It's not unusual nowadays to enter a croft house and find it occupied by an ecologist with his own internet web site, giving advice to someone in Saskatchewan.

Culture

It may sometimes strike the observer that the Scots have done a great job in managing to have things both ways. They are British when it suits them but also thoroughly Scots. This is nowhere more true than in their culture, which comes in two quite different forms. One is the shared cultural background of western Europe and with it the world-wide resources of the English language. The Scots' contribution to this wider culture is fairly modest compared to the major part they have played in the development of science, industry and modern ways of thinking, but it is not negligible – least of all to the Scots themselves.

> **The Scots' contribution to the wider culture of western Europe is modest but not negligible – least of all to the Scots themselves.**

The other element is the indigenous culture of Scotland itself. Inextricably tangled up though it is with tourist propaganda, at its heart it is still real and vibrant. Recollection of their Celtic heritage reminds the Scots that they have a soulful, spiritual side. They are prone to a sort of pleasantly wistful melancholia, especially when the skies are grey, or the days are at their shortest, or Scotland has just lost an international football game.

Scottish music

The fiddle, the piano accordion and the bagpipe form the basis of Scottish music, along with modern synthesisers and sound machines deplored by the purists. Aly Bain, the Shetland fiddler, has an international following, and he is one of a long line of highly accomplished Scottish fiddlers. Up to a thousand fiddlers may gather together for special performances.

> **66 Recollection of their Celtic heritage reminds the Scots that they have a soulful, spiritual side. 99**

But the listeners far outnumber the players, and radio programmes such as *Take theh Floor* featuring Scottish Country Dance music gain large audiences. The Scots like to see and hear their national cultural heritage, rather than actively participate in it. And of course they consider themselves excellent judges. When one piper got up to play at a concert in Skye, a member of the audience shouted: "Sit down, ye useless cratur (creature)." The chairman rose to protest: "Who called the piper a useless cratur?" Back came the reply: "Who called the useless cratur a piper?"

The Scots have invented a form of music all their own, the 'great music' of the pibroch, played solo on the

> **66** Scots like to see and hear their national cultural heritage, rather than participate in it. **99**

bagpipes. Composed according to strict rules of form and structure, it is the supreme test of a piper, and annual championships are held. Although open to players from all nations, this is a global trophy that stays firmly in Scotland.

Musicologists have detected a primitive element in the pentatonic scale of typical Scottish tunes that links them to a pre-Celtic, prehistoric musical tradition found also in Siberia and Mongolia. 'When we sing 'Auld Lang Syne',' wrote one, 'we may be perpetuating the melodic conventions of the Circumpolar Stone Age.' Such a thought would give great satisfaction to the Scots.

Literature

Life in old-time Scotland being distinctly short on home comforts, the country's early fiction writers like Robert Louis Stevenson tended to turn away from bleak reality to the more agreeable land of fantasy such as Treasure Island. The novels of Walter Scott reinvented a harsh and bloody history as something colourful, dramatic and heroic.

66 **The novels of Walter Scott reinvented a harsh and bloody history as something colourful, dramatic and heroic.** 99

These days it's New Realism. The lives of the unemployed, the drop-outs and the disaffected elements of city life in Glasgow and Edinburgh – lapped in a culture of drugs, drink and crime – have, ironically, made some writers of the 'bad boy' school famous and even wealthy. The irony is not lost on the writers themselves, like Irvine Welsh, whose Trainspotting brought Edinburgh into the international eye as something more than a gracious city of festival and flowers. Many Scots were surprised that a book (and film) with such remorselessly Scots dialogue as:

"Wuv goat that cairry-oot tae organise, mind."

"Aye, right. What ye gittin?"

"Boatil ay voddy 'n a few cans."

could be a world-wide hit.

The vigour of the new Scots fiction comes from tapping into the underlying contentiousness that forms one strand of the national character that emerges in violence and aggressive behaviour. Its subject matter also appears exotic – a culture not quite like any other. To an international public hungry for novelty, it is an exciting new taste.

Meanwhile, the genre of realistic, gritty writing typified by the Edinburgh-based crime novels of Ian Rankin has led to a reincarnation of tartan – 'tartan noir'.

Exiles and stay-at-homes

Some Scottish writers, like the Orcadian, George Mackay Brown, and the great Gaelic poet, Sorley Maclean, who was a teacher in Wester Ross, achieved wide success while remaining part of their own locality. But it is striking that many renowned Scottish creative artists moved out of Scotland, like Edinburgh-born novelist Muriel Spark, who set up home in Tuscany; and fashion designer Jean Muir who lived in London. Robert Louis Stevenson went as far away as he possibly could, to Samoa in the South Pacific, and then spent a large part of his time lying on his verandah among the palm trees, dreaming of, and re-creating, the Scotland of his youth.

> **❝ Robert Louis Stevenson spent much of his time in Samoa lying under the palm trees, dreaming of, and re-creating the Scotland of his youth. ❞**

Scotland produces two kinds of creative artists – those who are nourished by living there, and those who are stifled. Even those who remain are often rebels and liable to be deemed eccentrics, like 'concrete poet' Ian Hamilton Finlay, whose sculpture-poetry park is more honoured in Europe and America than in his home country, where he fought a lengthy battle with the authorities to secure its existence.

> **Scotland's greatest 20th-century poet got so far up the noses of the burghers of his birthplace they refused to put up a memorial to him.**

The prime example, however, is Scotland's greatest 20th-century poet, Hugh MacDiarmid, who got so far up the noses of the burghers of Langholm, his birthplace, that they refused to put up a memorial to him after his death.

Scottish artists often experience a lack of appreciation in their own country. It stems from a peculiar reluctance of the Scots to grant any special qualities to those who, in their opinion, have no right to be considered any better or more successful than anyone else. It is an attitude neatly summed up in the words "I kenned his faither".

Government

Parliament

Nearly 300 years after their parliament voted to abolish itself in a union with England, the Scots voted to have it back again. Established in 1999, parliament houses 129 members, who do not divide on the conventional left versus right model. Instead, three centre-left parties compete to form the Scottish Executive, as the government is officially called. The point of division is nationalism. The Scottish National Party (SNP) pushes for complete political separation from England. Labour and the Liberal Democrats favour the current arrangement of limited self-government, as do the small group of Conservatives.

Most aspects of home policy are controlled by the parliament, and although its economic powers are strictly limited, significant differences from English practice are emerging, especially in welfare and education. It has three languages: English (in which all its business is done), Gaelic, and Scots, and publishes a web site in each. In Scots you receive a warm 'Walcome til the Scottish Pairlament wabsite'.

Devolution is a relatively new experience for the Scots, who were previously free to criticise the shortcomings of

66 Nearly 300 years after their Parliament voted to abolish itself in a union with England, the Scots voted to have it back again. **99**

the English-dominated parliament in London for not listening to their needs. Now that the power to change things lies in their own hands, the criticism is focused on aspects of their own parliament, including the salaries and comforts of the members, and sometimes their pretensions to special importance – something that cannot be countenanced.

The electoral system for the Scottish parliament has been cunningly worked out to make it difficult for any party to have an absolute majority. Coalition governments are almost inevitable, making a new order of things for politicians. In the first session of the parliament this did not prevent the coalition partners branding each other as liars. But as coalition politics becomes the norm, politicians from opposing parties may even have to start listening to each other.

> **The electoral system for the Scottish parliament has been cunningly worked out to make it difficult for any party to have an absolute majority.**

Administration

Democracy weighs heavily on the Scots. Five tiers of administration are piled above them: the district council, the regional council, the Scottish parliament, the British parliament, and the European Union and its parliament. At least three different voting systems are in use. The Scots need to keep their wits about them just to make sure they vote for the person they really want.

> **Democracy weighs heavily on the Scots. Five tiers of administration are piled above them.**

In rural areas, local politics are decorous, on the surface at least, but elsewhere things can get heated.

The Lord Provost of Glasgow once had to barricade himself in his opulent office against furious members of his own party, and the burgh (town) council of Paisley became a source of national entertainment when feuding Labour and Nationalist members traded insults, bringing the playground phrase 'ya bampot' (you numbskull) to unaccustomed prominence.

Councils are viewed with suspicion. At the heart of this is the feeling that it may not be the desire to serve that motivates all local councillors. Scottish tribalism means that individuals or political parties can remain entrenched in powerful positions for a long time and begin to believe they are 'chiefs' by right rather than by permission. And chiefs have always dispensed favours to their faithful followers.

> **Individuals or political parties can remain entrenched in powerful positions for a long time and begin to believe they are 'chiefs' by right rather than by permission.**

Curiously, despite all the layers of government, much of the country's affairs are managed by unelected 'quangos' (quasi-autonomous non-governmental organisations). These bodies, which range from the an arts funding committee to area health authorities and water boards, spend vast sums of public money. Although run by professionals, they are controlled by political appointees from among what is casually referred to as 'the great and the good' ('great' at getting, 'good' at keeping). Opportunities for quiet chicanery are observed with cynicism by the population at large who don't themselves have access to expense accounts and celebratory lunches.

Law

The law is yet another area where Scots rejoice in their difference. In the Union of Scotland with England, the law and the Church were exempted from amalgamation with their English counterparts, and Scottish law remains distinct, closer to the Roman Law of continental Europe than to English Common Law.

The country is divided into sheriffdoms, with the sheriff, a qualified lawyer, able to try all but the gravest cases. These go to the Court of Session which is based in Edinburgh but travels on circuit to the major towns. Eminent as they are, the judges of this highest court cannot emulate the flamboyant behaviour of such 18th-century predecessors as Lord Braxfield and his colleagues, who thought nothing of calling for bottles of port to sustain them through a long trial.

> **There are some specific Scottish offences, like 'hamesucken', which means breaking into a man's house in order to beat him up.**

Each area court has its Procurator Fiscal, or examining magistrate. The courts still have the unique verdict, 'Not Proven', at their disposal, which lets an accused person go free but with the clear inference that they are not necessarily not guilty.

In Scottish law, you are assumed to be your own person, and to attempt suicide is not a crime. There are also some quite specific Scottish offences, like 'hamesucken', which means breaking into a man's house in order to beat him up.

Scottish law produces some colourful figures, especially among advocates (Scottish barristers), some of whom rely on personality and oratory, as much as the facts, to sway a jury. One such, having

> 66 The courts still have the unique verdict, 'Not Proven', which lets an accused person go free but with the clear inference that they are not necessarily not guilty. 99

by impassioned pleading secured a 'Not Guilty' verdict for a known felon, was congratulated afterwards by his client with the words: "You almost had me convinced of my own innocence."

Royalty

Scotland is a kingdom, one of the oldest in Europe. Its crown and sceptre – known as the Honours of Scotland – are on display in Edinburgh Castle. It was a Scottish king, James VI, who went to London in 1603 to become king of England as well, as James I.

Scots like to remind folk that their monarch is

queen, or king, of Scots – not of Scotland: a leader of the people, not the owner of the land. Mixed in with the nationalist and left-wing orientation of Scottish politics is a strong republican streak. The popularity

> **66** An element is said to exist whose slogan is: 'Sean Connery for King'. **99**

of the royal family waxes and wanes, and they are seen as visitors rather than part of the fabric of the country. The royal Palace of Holyroodhouse is empty for much of the year. But for most Scots, especially when they look around at their elected representatives and speculate on how any of them would perform as president, the question of monarchy versus republic is not a live issue, even though an element is said to exist whose slogan is: 'Sean Connery for King'.

Language

Scots and English

The Scots once spoke a distinct kind of English, called Scots, and to many outsiders it seems they still do. In fact, today the Scots speak standard English – more or less, and what is left of the Scots language is now an endangered species, to the point that schools, which once tried to beat it out of children, now have it on the curriculum as a special subject.

Even modern poems written in Scots are published

with glossaries to explain such phrases as: 'Bumpity doun in the corrie gaed whuddran the pitiless whunstane'. (The pitiless whinstone went rushing bumpily down into the mountain hollow.)

Scots speech is garnished with words that are exclusively and distinctively Scots. Most are expressive. Even a Sassenach (the Gaelic term for 'Saxon') has no trouble in understanding what is meant by 'dreich' weather, or its opposite, a 'braw' day. A 'snell' wind is one that penetrates, and a 'gurly' sea is not for pleasure trips. To be 'couthy' is to be the salt of the earth, a bit rough and ready perhaps, but that's almost a virtue. To keep a 'trig' house means it's properly neat and tidy, but a lady who hears herself

> **A 'snell' wind is one that penetrates, and a 'gurly' sea is not for pleasure trips.**

defined as 'perjink' has been found to be just a bit too fastidious, although this is better than being 'clarty', or dirty, or being the kind of slovenly woman dismissed as 'just a gether-up'. Anything that is a regular nuisance is a perfect 'scunner'.

The old tongue reaches deep into the Scottish psyche, and Scots words leap to the lips in moments of stress or emotion. Lovers are 'dearies'. Children are 'weans' and 'bairns'. Silly people are 'numpties', while a person of common sense has 'smeddum' or 'mense'. The pale and sickly are said to look 'peeliewally', the day-dreamer is in a 'dwam', someone with too much to do is 'trachled', and if everything is too much, he might go clean 'gyte'. Even the word 'not' becomes 'nae' in Scots, as in this ditty about Scottish wool: 'It keeps it shape, it aims to please; you'll nae see sheep with baggy knees.'

While many Scots words are common to the whole nation, others are used only in certain districts and instantly show where the speaker comes from. Thus in the north-east, laddies and lassies become 'loons' and 'quines'. In all parts there is regular use of the Scottish diminutive. 'Wee' is a much loved word, and the -ie ending is often thrown in for good measure. A wee loonie in Aberdeen is not a vertically challenged madman but a little boy.

> **A wee loonie in Aberdeen is not a vertically challenged madman but a little boy.**

Take note that there is little point in practising phrases such as 'It's a braw, bricht, moonlicht nicht, the nicht, the noo', or 'There's a moose loose aboot this hoose', as you will find it is virtually impossible to fit them into any conversation.

Scottish accents communicate a range of values. Telephone sales companies like to employ speakers with what they call an 'educated Scots' accent. Its clarity and precision give their message an aura of reliability and sincerity, and polls have shown that it is the most trusted accent in Britain.

However, Scottish accents vary greatly around the

country. From the mouth of a Glaswegian, for instance, a declaration of love can sound like a death threat. From the native of a Hebridean island, a death threat can sound like poetry. Strangely enough the accents all sound Scottish (even the Aberdonians', and not even the Scots understand what they are saying).

Those who are not themselves from Glasgow find a guide to Glasgow-speak very useful, and *Parliamo Glasgow*, with its explanations of such useful phrases as: JAWANNABEELTOANRAMOOTH? ('Do you want a belt on the mouth?'), is never out of print.

The *Gaedhealtachd*

As you cross the Highland line, you will encounter daunting notices in Gaelic welcoming you to the *Gaedhealtachd* ('Country of the Gaels'). But unless you venture to the Outer Hebrides, your chance of hearing Gaelic spoken as an everyday language is pretty remote. Gaelic is spoken by less than 100,000 of the population. The last person to speak nothing but Gaelic died early in the 20th century.

> **Unless you venture to the Outer Hebrides, your chance of hearing Gaelic spoken as an everyday language is pretty remote.**

Six hundred years ago Gaelic was the language of the entire country, except for Anglo-Saxon Lothian. It has been fighting a lengthy rearguard action. But just before it is too late, and the language is lost for ever, there has been some recognition that a huge part of Scottish history and culture is wrapped up in the Gaelic language, and to lose that would be like losing half the country's identity. Hundreds of years of Scotland's past are preserved in Gaelic, a living language which more than 98% of Scots do not understand. It is like being in a house with a locked-up room that is never referred to, and to which some elderly and undesirable relative has been banished.

> **In the Highlands a generation ago, parents used to speak Gaelic for not-in-front-of-the-children topics.**

Nor does it relate only to the culture of bygone and very different times. Some of Scotland's finest modern poetry is in Gaelic. While it is never likely to be an everyday language again, there is a resurgence of Gaelic teaching and writing. In the Highlands, a generation ago, parents used to speak Gaelic for delicate, not-in-front-of-the-children topics. Now the children, profiting from Gaelic classes at school, do the same with subjects they deem unsuitable for adult ears.

The Author

David Sutherland Ross is a fully fledged member of that well-established species, the Scottish literary exile. Born in Oban, Argyll, and furnished with a Scottish education, he migrated to London intending to become a journalist, but became a publisher instead.

Having learned from writing blurbs for other people's books how to represent a tangle of ill-assorted elements and random events as a unified whole, he was eminently qualified to write a history of Scotland. The outcome was Scotland: History of a Nation. He went on to become a full-time writer and compiler of anthologies, including Awa' and Bile Yer Heid, a collection of Scottish insults and invective described as 'rich and ripe offensiveness'. Its success assures him of a pile all to himself in Scottish bookshops.

The Americans

The American language embraces the bias towards good feelings. Stocks that plummet to half their value aren't losers, they're 'non-performers'. Someone doesn't have a near brush with death; he or she has a 'life-affirming experience'.

The Greeks

The ancient sages saw fit to carve their maxims 'Nothing in excess' and 'Know thyself' on the portals of the Delphic Oracle, in an attempt to persuade their fellow Greeks to curb their emotions. They were not heeded then any more than they are now.

The Kiwis

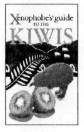

To Kiwis, politeness is synonymous with warmth and generosity of spirit. Thus North Islanders, when complimented by visitors on their scenery, will ask anxiously, "But have you seen the South Island yet?" They do not want to be seen as hogging the best bits for themselves.

The Swedes

The Swedes brood a lot over the meaning of life in a self-absorbed way without ever arriving at satisfactory answers. Literature offers few clues, and the news media even fewer. There is a secret entrance, however, in the form of Swedish cinema.

The French

French politicians look smart because power itself is chic, attractive, seductive, and one should dress to look the part. The French electorate would never allow any government to intervene in their lives if it were shabbily dressed.

The Canadians

The Canadian attitude to the cold is an admirable show of good faith – mostly in the down filling of one's parka. Canadians tend to look down on anyone who says he can't handle the cold, and like to think that extreme weather conditions build character.

On the series:

"A series which takes a light-hearted look at the residents of various countries without crossing the fine line between funny and cruel."   *North of Scotland Newspapers*

The Germans:

"An excellent cross-cultural guide. Enjoy a chuckle as you focus on the endearing foibles and frustrating traits of one of the most interesting peoples in the world. Must read for anyone contemplating studying, living or working in Deutschland."

Reader from Frankfurt

The Icelanders:

"Fantastic portrayal of a nation. I'm Icelandic myself and everything this book states is completely correct and a greatly humorous view of the nation."

Reader from Reykjavik, Iceland

The Poles:

"What superb insight, what humour – but of course written by a Pole. This is well worth a read and I am buying several to put in relation's Christmas stockings."

Reader from Essex, England

Xenophobe's® guides

Xenophobe's® lingo learners

66 Speak the lingo by speaking English. 99

Xenophobe's® Guides

Xenophobe's® Guides are available
as e-books from Amazon, iBookstore, and
other online sources, and via:

www.xenophobes.com

Xenophobe's® Guides print versions
can be purchased through online retailers
(Amazon, etc.) or via our web site:

www.xenophobes.com

In the US contact:
IPG Trafalgar Square, Chicago

toll free no: 1-800-888-4741
e-mail: orders@ipgbook.com

In the UK, contact Oval Books, London

telephone: +44 (0)20 7733 8585
e-mail: info@ovalbooks.com

Oval Books
5 St John's Buildings
Canterbury Crescent
London SW9 7QH

Oval Books accepts Visa and Mastercard and offers
FREE packing and postage on orders of more than
one book (to one address).